'Andrew is both a critical and reflective thinker and he encourages people to develop the skills and strategies to enable them to increase the probability of a desirable outcome in life. He promotes thinking that is purposeful, both reasoned and goal directed. Andrew's book assists the reader to use their reflective thinking skills to be aware of and control their lives by assessing what they know, what they need to know and how to bridge the void between the two. Readers are challenged to examine their traditional thinking and to charter new oceans of reasoning.'

Peter Meaney
Head of Education, Royal Melbourne Institute of Technology

'Andrew is a truly genuine man with a passion for learning and developing people in ways that sustain them. He is a clear thinker, forthright, honest and a great listener. His insights are enlightening and delivered in a considered way. In my experience he has always striven to improve and build on systems to support others. I have appreciated his friendship and support for many years.'

Michael White
Director, Manager Learning & Development, Industry Training Board

'Andrew is a man of acute insight. He has a passion in assisting people achieve excellence and maximize all the possibilities that they are capable, providing drive and empowerment in seeing people live to their full potential in life. Andrew has created a book that will help us all move to a life of fullness and deep satisfaction; I want it with me everywhere I go. It lifts me up and inspires me to live a life of greatness that I am capable of, if my thinking is right.

Peter Leggett
Managing Director, Arrive Wealth Management

Published by Brolga Publishing Pty Ltd
ABN 46 063 962 443
PO Box 12544, A'Beckett Street,
Melbourne, Victoria, Australia, 8006

email: bepublished@brolgapublishing.com.au
web: www.brolgapublishing.com.au

All rights reserved. No part of this publication may be reproduced, stored in a retrieval system or transmitted in any form or by any means electronic, mechanical, photocopying, recording or otherwise without prior permission from the publisher.

Copyright © Andrew Horsfield 2007

National Library of Australia
Cataloguing-in-Publication entry

Horsfield, Andrew, 1971- .
Check up from the neck up : unlock the power of your true self.

ISBN 9781921221286 (pbk.).

1. Motivation (Psychology). 2. Self-help techniques. I. Title.

153.8

Printed in Singapore
Cover Design by David Khan
Typeset by David Khan & Imogen Stubbs

Check Up from the Neck Up

Andrew Horsfield

Acknowledgements

The quotations in this book have been gathered lovingly but unscientifically over several years and contributions from many sources, friends or acquaintances. Some arrived, and survived in files or on scraps of paper and therefore may have come imperfectly worded or attributed. To the authors, contributors and original sources, thanks, and where appropriate, apologies.

Special Thanks

Mandy Berry your ideas, effort and conversations have been exceptionally helpful in creating, refining and designing these pages. Thank you for the time, titles and most importantly, friendship over the years. To Gary Udal, Russell Saunders, Peter Meaney and Michael and Jo Hansen for complete friendship that I absolutely value and will always work to strengthen and maintain. DtC - our constant conversations, companionship and occasional jocularity keeps mates at hand and my mind engaged. Last and by no means least the people who read preliminary pages, gave honest and open feedback and either directly or indirectly influenced the final product.

Thanks

Say it ⟶ **Mean it** ⟶ **Live it**

1st & 4most

Thanks to my parents, Rod and Beth, for overwhelming support, great lessons in life and most importantly for the stuff they did which I still don't know about.

Great people, great teachers and great friends.

To you for picking up this book. You are now helping me fulfill a dream and hopefully through these pages will realise, appreciate and create your own.

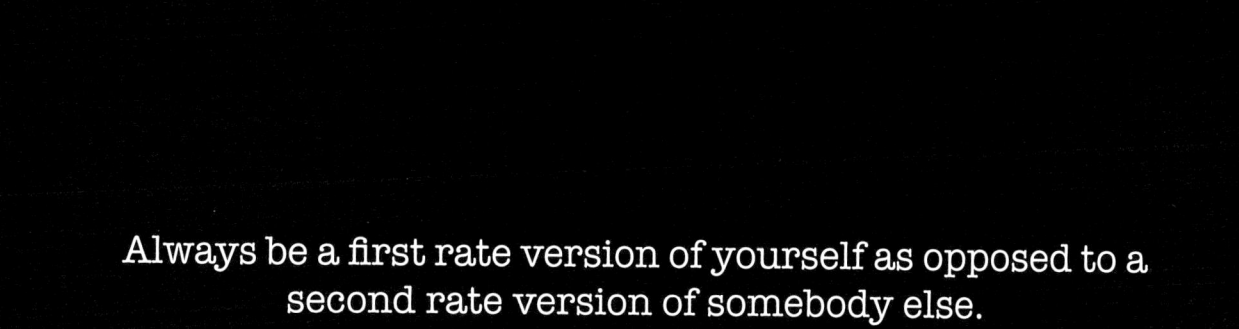
Always be a first rate version of yourself as opposed to a second rate version of somebody else.

Shut up or eat up?

You are out with good friends and just received a meal that isn't to your complete satisfaction. Do you immediately call for the waiter, make a comment to your friends or 'eat up' guzzling wine to wash down the less than perfect meal?

Your response to this question is not life threatening (presuming of course you are at a reputable restaurant!) however, it gives direct insight into who you are. No one answer is correct or more right than another as it is purely personal preference – yet here is the catch:

Do you completely understand why you made your choice?

On a surface level people often proffer a straightforward answer that, not being in the situation, completely contradicts what they would do when actually confronted with the circumstance. Not dissimilar to the responses people offer when asked what would they do if they won a million dollars and they promise to look after family, donate to charity or those less fortunate and then spend on themselves – often in that order.

Easy to respond and divide up when it isn't actually sitting in a bank account with friends, family and long distance relatives calling with congratulations and dinner invitations.

If you are being true to yourself and your own beliefs why would the response potentially change from one situation to another?

Adding to the complexity would be exploring a response if the situation were a work function, involved the in-laws rather than good friends or perhaps being on a first date with someone you are keen to know better.

Would your response differ in any of these situations?

If you are being true to yourself and your own beliefs why would the response potentially change from one situation to another?

Quite simply because in life we are often tangled in our thoughts to please or over accommodate others, we make decisions based upon what is socially acceptable or to 'fit in' and present ourselves based upon others' views and expectations. Do you know:

- ❖ A young adult who has to have all the latest computer games or fashionable clothes?

- ❖ A parent who constantly and without question will always put the family's needs before their own?

- ❖ Colleagues who will work back late on request (although under sufferance) due to others poor organisation or planning?

- ❖ People who enact being someone else to meet a socially desirable stereo type or to 'fit in' their social network?

All of these situations involve making personal choices and often the choice people make is not always the one that they desire. Yet for some strange reason, people continue to put themselves in situations that make them unhappy and unfulfilled; and that slowly erodes energy, self worth and personal success in the process.

That is where the idea for this book came into being. I thought it important for people to understand more of themselves as a way of finding a path to a stronger sense of self, a feeling of enhanced happiness and ultimately personal success. Success because finding and valuing your true sense of self will help guide and determine your future choices which in turn will determine your personal contribution and what you have in life.

So it begs the question from the previously stated examples, what need is being fulfilled for someone who goes against what they feel like or really want to do when making choices? Some possibilities may include the need to be accepted, being concerned about appearances, avoiding being offensive or an argument, deciding to put another's needs above your own or an inability to confront difficulty or possible conflict.

The reasons are numerous and varied, however the point is relatively simple. Are you cognizant of what drives your choices and more importantly, are you making decisions or undertaking 'vanillacide' in your life through decision making processes bereft of what you actually think, feel, believe and value. Are your decisions and approach to life working for you or against you?

Of course the intent and aspiration of this book needs to be put in context of being part of and recognizing a sense of family, community and society. You will have noticed Gordon Gecko from Wall Street fame has not written a forward.

Creating a stronger sense of you is about growing strength internally. Although endorsing a strong understanding of self to ensure you are mindful of where your choices and actions are ultimately helping or hindering you, this does not mean in complete isolation or exercising power over others.

Personal power and confidence does not mean at Dr Evil (Austen Powers' arch nemesis) proportions! That is – ultimate control where you move to an exotic island with your favorite pet as a side-kick to plot taking over the world!

My aspiration is to engage you as a reader in active thought and exploration about understanding who you really are and what you stand for through your actions and the decisions you make. Recognising of course this will sometimes be a decision that is made for yourself and at other times made with your needs parked behind something or someone else.

Therefore, how you present yourself, the decisions you make and outcomes you achieve in your life are aligned to the person you want to be and not weighed down being everything to everyone but in the end – nothing to yourself.

So… enjoy the pages of this book. They have been designed for you to explore, read randomly, reflect upon, talk about with friends, share with colleagues, even store next to the toilet and read. Although the book can be read from cover to cover in one easy sitting if you are in a comfy chair, I also hope you flick through pages randomly and continue to interact with these ideas. Over time perspective changes and the way you see the page initially will be different to the way you see it with future flicks!

Take moments in time however you decide to read this book to explore your sense of self and understand your deeper workings. In doing so you will have germinated seeds that will grow and help you truly blossom as a person.

Reading, reflecting, and where necessary taking action, will hopefully enable you to become someone who you can be truly honest with and feel proud through creating and refining your distinctive sense of self.

What's in it for me?

This book will not provide neatly packaged absolute answers for your life. I have, in fact, worked hard to abstain from a self help genre and ensure neat answers don't happen!

The intention is to promote a sense of mindfulness to help you better understand how the way you see and interact with the world directly impacts your life. With an enhanced understanding of this connection I believe you will be more educated about your mind's habits providing openness to its routines. These are the routines that generate your decisions, direct your journey and ultimately determine your destination.

> **To exist is to change, to change is to mature,**
> **to mature is to go on creating oneself endlessly.**
> **Henri Bergson**

Awareness of your mind's habits and how these habits impact on the way you interrelate with the world enables a creation as opposed to a reaction to life. A greater sense of mindfulness allows for new perspectives and approaches to be considered and attempted. This ensures a larger behavioural toolbox is accessed to gain the most effective outcomes for situations and scenarios you encounter.

To encourage your journey I have dedicated each page to exploring YOU in more detail. Having the courage to be open to knowing how you either help or hinder your current sense of self, and the way you engage with other people and life, is a great starting point for turning the page. I invite you to turn the page, read and contemplate.

ENJOY!

Andrew's Journey

I started working life as a school teacher trying my very best to engage young learners and impart some wisdom throughout the years in which they skipped, scurried or were dragged into the classroom.

Confession up front – as a young teacher straight out of university a lot of that wisdom was initially what the text books and teachers notes taught me. As I grew as an educator however, so did my confidence and ability to utilize my own life skills & experiences to engage and educate people rather than teach. Tapping into the rich experience, knowledge & skills of others generates energy.

Learning at this point for me then became more about asking questions and discovery through life experience, shared learning and trial and error as opposed to finding it in a textbook. When engaged in true open learning I found the process to be humbling while at the same time very inspirational. Teaching with heart gave me heart.

There is a certain freedom in allowing yourself to be driven by the process of inquiry rather than having the answer, exploring and working with personal vulnerability and always being honest with yourself to capture truly effective and empowering insights.

This is something that I have a passion for and drives me daily. I hope in the pages of this book you also find that freedom.

Who do you think you are?

How well do you truly know yourself? Your level of self awareness about who you are and what you stand for provides great personal insight. How you feel in a particular situation will determine your level of engagement in that event and consequently help or hinder you achieve what you desire. Event to event, day to day and as a natural progression - through your life.

There are many circumstances where people's thoughts and feelings control the outcome in any given situation: people's reactions when confronting change, their response when asked to give a speech or their attitude when caught in heavy traffic just to name a few. Who you are and how you choose to think and engage in any of these situations will go a long way to determining the outcome you experience.

The following pages are created to promote a sense of self awareness. Knowing who you are is the foundation stone for the behavior you choose to adopt, decisions you make and the outcomes you ultimately encounter. Without self awareness people often fail to see other perspectives or possibilities. They consume their own thinking with blame, denial or justification for actions, unaware of the connection between themselves and outcomes they experience.

So flick through the pages that have been created, reflect upon who you are and contemplate how you engage with life. I truly hope the times you are being extraordinary are highlighted and room for new understanding, approaches and growth are unearthed.

Is this reflective of your approach to life?

Before you tuck into this book too deeply...

Place the book on your lap, gaze into the distance and think about the question opposite.

Right now with where you are in your life, the decisions you are making and day to day actions you are taking; do you feel a sense of purpose or a sense of drift?

What is it that you actually want to create for yourself?

By choice or by chance?

We all make choices and receive particular impacts from those choices. Some are exceptionally positive and others frustrate and torment us to the point where we break, give up or respond poorly to others.

Some people believe that life just is what it is or there are certain circumstances out of their control. There are elements of truth to that perspective. Relating to your own happiness and life's success however, regardless of how that is measured, living through choice as opposed to chance has a far higher probability of you achieving your dreams.

Think for a minute.

How often do you own and acknowledge your choices and accept that your decisions directly impact on your actions and consequently what you get in life?

Understanding and appreciating how choices relate to outcomes provides people with an opportunity to create the life they desire through the choices they make. This doesn't imply that it always works out the way you want OR doesn't involve set backs and new learning.

Being on a creative path however, empowers you to create your life and the future or particular outcomes you desire and not be at the whim of others or certain circumstances happening in order to achieve your outcome.

The perspective of living by choice reflects a creative orientation and bringing something that you want into being. Life becomes a journey where obstacles presented are viewed as opportunities for new perspective and personal growth. The alternative is seeing problems, constant hurdles and reasons why things are not as you want them to be.

With the focus being on the problems and not the possibilities the view is very different. Seeing your existence as problems, what's going wrong, why things are not as they should be, erodes energy, creativity, and ultimately desire.

The alternative possesses energy, drive, determination and an enjoyment in pursuing a future result or outcome. Ultimately, enjoying the journey, not solely the destination.

What is your view and approach to life creating for you?

Is this the way

you see the world?

When was the last time you genuinely considered, undertook or embraced a different perspective?

There are many ways to see and take hold of the world.

What!?
Didn't believe me?

You are now seeing something in the world from a different perspective. Sure, I could have said this page was a mistake from the printing apprentice who put the book together - but it's not. It is meant to be upside down to show you how easy it is to gain a different perspective.

Does it always work? No. Do you sometimes feel uncomfortable? Yes. Will your life be more engaging and fulfilling? Absolutely.

Order different food when you go out to a restaurant, try a different coffee at the café, sit in a different seat on the train, read a different genre of book or simply do anything that defies your 'usual way'.

The additional purpose of this page is to get you thinking about how easy your actions are to take. You could just read this book but to get your money's worth take some action. Write notes somewhere, keep a journal, talk to a friend or share the book with colleagues and discuss a particular page over coffee once a week. Doesn't matter really.

What matters is that in promoting your thinking, you also capture that opportunity to turn your thinking into action. Finding distinction in this book and your life is paying attention to things that provoke your thinking. Find your own way of capturing them, contemplating their meaning and deciding what action you will take.

Do that and you will bring out the awesome potential that exists in you!

Live daringly, boldly and fearlessly.
Put forth the best within you.

Make Your Mark

It is worth mentioning early something about personal change.

The world is full of people who know what isn't working for them, ultimately desire change and yet somehow remain stagnant not knowing what to do or how to effect that change.

Personal development and growth takes courage and persistence because there is often vulnerability and risk associated.

To reach and understand the fundamental reasons for desiring change takes self exploration, uncovering the source of true values and beliefs, what you think and feel 'deep down' and being prepared to confront new possibilities in the way you see and interact with the world.

Why is this hard? Because we make sense of the world by labeling things. This is the basis for our communication and helps to give each of us a framework to exist.

It has also been the foundation in our minds responsible for choosing particular behaviour in the past that has shaped our experiences.

Each of those good experiences, by human nature we want to repeat to have more good experiences. The issue arises when we confront the tension of learning or having to do something new.

What was once easy or in your capability to manage now presents a sense of uneasiness and perhaps even difficulty.

The response is often to return to the familiar habits and approaches that relieve the existing tension being felt.

Unfortunately this only compounds the issue as old habits are not always the most appropriate; just comfortable.

The opportunity in this book is for you to discover the areas of your life that need a new coat of paint, render or in some circumstances, a complete knock down rebuild.

In living your life today, and continuing the same routines, habits and behaviours, justifying to yourself why there is just one way, perspective or truth is limiting.

One of the great opportunities in life is to create a magnificent journey. Welcoming new opportunities and as a consequence creating different experiences and opportunities for learning.

Just like a fingerprint, your mark, impact on others and ability to shape your own future and life outcome is personal; and up to you to drive.

As you read or flick through this book think about your responses to the pages. Be aware of what is being created in your mind, discover where it is generated from and where appropriate, celebrate your attitude and approach or start the thinking process for embracing and attempting change.

Should something resonate with you and you decide to make a change remember; it will be tough, challenge will have to be confronted and overcome and your own self confidence may at times be dented.

The brave we know may not live forever, however the cautious never live at all. Take on life.

My sister recently visited for a holiday and we ventured down the coast. On arriving at our destination we opened the windows to let the fresh air, sunshine, sounds and smells of the sea engulf what had been a stale room.

Our minds and the way we live life, just like the window, also needs to be cranked open occasionally. Not exposing the mind to new ideas, opinions, possibilities and reality also makes for a stale room!

Past experiences give wisdom. Forgetting to reality check that wisdom however, living solely from your past and what worked before is limiting. Just like a colleague I once taught with who professed she had been teaching for 20 years. In fact, all she had been doing was repeating her first experience (yes, including the exact same lesson plans!) 19 times over!

Our mind is something we take with us every day, into every situation and circumstance as the main control room. Control it, and you will go a fair distance to controlling your life.

How often do you pay attention to and understand what you think, why you think it and whether it is actually working for you? Let alone bring those thoughts together to identify recurring patterns and complexities to truly be in a place to manage your mind.

How you think about things impacts your emotions and approach which in turn dictates the outcomes in your life. A study on 'lucky people' conducted in the UK over a ten year period showed people who are lucky have no more or less opportunity than other people.

A $5 note was placed on the footpath and those considered lucky saw and picked up the note where those considering themselves unlucky walked straight past it! What we tell our mind when formulating its program (yes we actually are responsible for that!) will be the outlook that plays out in our lives. In a nutshell, being lucky is no more than a mindset.

So… find your inner 'humana humana' and get in touch with the programs you are setting. Your mindset is the barometer for how life will be for you so if you are not feeling fulfilled and content; re-program your bonse and master your mind.

How can I start to master my mind?

Be affirming with yourself. Learn to see and appreciate the positive and glowing skills and traits you have and use each day.

Develop mindfulness around the messages you send to your mind. These messages create those programs that form how you see yourself and the world around you.

What are you telling yourself?

Here is a new opportunity for me to try
I am not very good at this

If I stuff this up my career is over
Here's my opportunity to influence key people

I'll never be able to/good at…
This is challenging for me right now

Develop positive self-talk where you send positive vibes and messages to your mind. Be committed to seeing the positive or opportunity in a situation and see how this simple technique makes a huge difference.

When something is difficult, hard or seemingly out of reach recognize that. Knowing how you feel and where you are, allows you to genuinely work out how to get to where you want to be. It's using the power of your emotions not ignoring them.

Smile! The attitude and behaviour you have is often reflected back to you. Get positive; exude energy and a positive outlook; you'll be surprised the difference it makes.

The mind is very powerful. Paying attention and understanding your thoughts, and ensuring they work in harmony with your life direction is critical to you getting there.

Master Your Mind!!

Reading and giving this page some time will be really difficult for some people. Quite simply because it takes quite a lot of thinking, reflection, vulnerability and most importantly, personal responsibility. Taking responsibility for the actions and outcomes in your life is one of the fundamental elements to happiness.

If you don't believe, don't see or don't want to take control and responsibility for your life then it will always be forever in the hands of someone or something else. Taking responsibility is difficult when colleagues, friends and common belief encourage us to find ways to divert poor judgment, bad decisions or questionable outcomes somewhere other than ourselves.

Check out the lists below to see the subtle yet powerful difference between being out of control and taking control. If you dare, think about the conversations, decisions and approaches you undertook in the past week to determine which side of the ledger you are sitting. If you are not satisfied with where you ended up make a change!

OUT OF CONTROL

Blame everything or everyone else for what is occurring, why it went wrong and how it impacts on you?

Provide **reasons** for why you didn't succeed, why circumstances are not as you'd like or why someone else is wrong.

Justify to yourself why situations 'are as they are' leaving no room for self reflection, learning or personal growth.

In extreme cases or when risks are high **deny** anything ever happened!

TAKING CONTROL

Find out what went wrong, why things are not working and help make them better.

Understand the reasons for the way things are; yet take responsibility for personal growth or creating possible solutions.

Admit a mistake, see another perspective or even adopt new techniques or behaviours that will get the result you desire.

Be open, brave and human enough to take responsibility and communicate how the issue can be addressed.

Are you:

a) Letting it happen?

b) Making it happen?

c) Wondering what happened?

If you think you are too small to be effective, you have **never** been in bed with a mosquito!

The right mind, matched with the right motivation can achieve anything.

What are you connecting with from your past experiences?

We all have a past...

Whether it is a sporting triumph, being teased at school, excelling at music or the arts or arguing with parents as a difficult teenager; our past experiences make up who we are today.

A tapestry of highs and lows, and triumphs and tragedies provide opportunities to learn, grow, celebrate success and overcome adversity on the dramatic stage of life.

Today, you are the culmination of your experiences. The good, the bad and the damn-right embarrassing! In fact, this is true not just from childhood but from your experiences last year, last month, even yesterday!

Absorbing the lows and celebrating the highs are what makes for an engaging and fruitful existence. Imagine if there was no uphill on the rollercoaster.

Do you know what experiences from your past now help you and hold you back in life?

Getting the best mark in a test that provided confidence at an early age amongst peers.

Forgetting your lines in the school play which made you afraid of public speaking or making presentations.

People loving your outfit on casual clothes day gave you self confidence about personal opinions and choices.

Turning up to school each day knowing that finding and keeping friends is a skill that you find really tough.

Receiving a pat on your back and small bonus from your boss for a job well done.

Understanding our strengths and areas of vulnerability is positive. This enables you to channel energy, manage, address or in extreme cases seek further help to deal with the difficulties of the past.

Allowing yourself to let go of the negative past, become focused on future possibility and opportunity is a key factor to achieving happiness.

The alternative is like carrying around a ball and chain of negative experiences that weigh you down, prevent freedom of movement and opportunity to truly access the potential in your life.

Talk to your friends from school, discuss your upbringing or difficulty with your family or share your horror stories and/or embarrassing moments with your closest friends or companion.

Do whatever you need to free yourself of your past and open up your future. The more space you open up the more that space can be filled with what you create in the here and now.

This is not necessarily an easy task or solved in one conversation or action.

One thing is for sure, you can not change the past only influence the future; and you certainly won't make a difference while staying stationary.

Go for a step change no matter how large or small and ensure that your future, the possibilities you see and life you embrace, is driven by where you are heading, not where you have been.

...& fortunately a future

Th!nk

Are you a person that allows yourself time to think?

Genuine time and space to think, reflect and contemplate whatever is important to you but disassociated to the immediate troubles, day to day timelines and/or confronting issues?

Much has been written about slowing down, reducing time creep, relaxing and ensuring that your mind can be engaged. You will be amazed how giving your mind some space can aid in creating new ideas, possibilities and outcomes for all areas of your life.

Think its all spin? Well as a bare minimum engage your thinking day to day by realising that not all ideas are outcomes, and not all possibilities become concrete decisions. Let your mind explore the full extent when contemplating new approaches, possibilities and different opinions.

What were you like at school?

Where will you be in five years?

If your house was burning to the ground what three things would you take?

What has been your most embarrassing moment in a social situation?

What would your closest friends say are your most admirable traits?

If you could make one sustainable change for the world, what would it be?

What is your dream job? Why?

Questions like these occur at dinner parties, on dates as people try and get to know each other as well as in the media for the quick celebrity interview.

How well you do you know yourself and, not necessarily to these questions, but answers to the questions that DO matter to you?

How do you communicate, live out and integrate the things that are important to you in your life? Are you consistent or do people, circumstances or other external factors get in the way?

Find a quiet space, prepare your mind and give yourself a Q&A session reflecting on the questions that ARE important to you. Alternatively; grab a friend, a good bottle of red and engage them in the conversation!

Big Rocks

One day an expert in time management was speaking to a group of business student's and, to drive home a point, used an illustration those students will never forget.

As he stood in front of the group of high powered overachievers he said, "Okay, time for a quiz." Then he pulled out a one-gallon, wide mouth Mason jar and set it on the table in front of him. Then he produced about a dozen fist-sized rocks and carefully placed them, one at a time, into the jar.

When the jar was filled to the top and no more rocks would fit inside, he asked, "Is this jar full?" Everyone in the class said, "Yes."

Then he said, "Really?" He reached under the table and pulled out a bucket of gravel. Then he dumped some gravel in and shook the jar causing pieces of gravel to work themselves down into the spaces between the big rocks.

Then he asked the group once more, "Is the jar full?" By this time, the class was on to him.

"Probably not," one of them answered. "Good!" he replied.

He reached under the table and brought out a bucket of sand. He started dumping the sand in the jar and it went into all of the spaces left between the rocks and the gravel.

Once more he asked the question, "Is this jar full?" "No!" the class shouted. Once again he said, "Good." Then he grabbed a pitcher of water and began to pour it in until the jar was filled to the brim. Then he looked at the class and asked, "What is the point of this illustration?"

One eager beaver raised his hand and said, "The point is, no matter how full your schedule is if you try really hard you can always fit some more things in it!"

"No," the speaker replied, "that's not the point. The truth this illustration teaches us is: If you don't put the big rocks in first, you'll never get them in at all.

What are the big rocks in your life?

Talk + Walk = True Values

Personal values are commonly defined as what is important to us. In society, for example, we value integrity because we see people with integrity as those who will take actions that benefit the larger whole. Some commonly espoused values include honesty, integrity, social responsibility, loyalty, justice, fairness and diversity.

Do you know what you value?

Of course you do! You have probably rattled off some of your 'big ticket' values automatically in your head just by reading that question. Where this equation becomes tricky however, is between the values we tell or espouse to others and the ones that our day to day actions and decisions show. What we say and what we actually do don't always align. Need some proof?

Valuing honesty but giving false opinions on fashion because a lot of effort has been made
Valuing physical health and well being but being a regular smoker
Valuing cooperation but resenting being asked to stay back one Friday evening to help out

So value is probably best defined by what guides our actions and reflects what is important than the definition provided earlier. This isn't just semantics either. Our actions reflect what is important to us; and when the set of values that is espoused is not demonstrated or aligned to the actions undertaken there is a gap.

The presence of this gap creates values conflicts by saying one thing but providing actions that do not match.

A phrase has even been invented to remind us to align what we say and what we do!

Walk the talk

This is not as easy as it seems for a number of good reasons.

❶ People have to know what they actually value - you'll find this out by paying attention to who or what your actions serve!

❷ Meeting values dilemmas head on – ensuring that what plays out in your life matches what's in your head!

❸ Most people don't know how to share their self serving values with other people – be honest, respectful of others and have a balance of self serving and enriching values.

❹ Cultural fit or assimilation exists in all sorts of circumstances - exercising values that differ or oppose 'the norm' is always challenging!

So why is all this important?

Your values are the rudder for your ship of choice that guides your actions and demonstrates what is important to you. Knowing what you value and living those values are the keys to many of life's great treasures including effective leadership, respect, trust, love, authenticity, admiration, spirituality, integrity, self expression, learning, empathy, kindness, altruism, a sense of community and so on and so on!

So having read that perspective it begs the question... do you know what you value?

Confidence is King

Elvis impersonators have a pretty tough time. Their lives are about emulating arguably the greatest rocker of all time with the largest fan base across the globe.

Elvis was King and consequently so must be the loyal men and women who today help his legend live on.

What's the secret weapon for the Elvis impersonator? Confidence.

The confidence factor for any performance or personality is largely related to success, a positive feeling and outlook on what we choose to engage in day to day - positive or otherwise.

How are your levels of confidence, the ability to identify and act upon opportunities or overcome obstacles?

If you are not demonstrating Elvis impersonator levels then take a closer look around the edges of this page and get busy!

Thank you. Thank you very much.

A lack of confidence is often nerves – take deep breaths and let O2 in! Work out what's sapping your confidence and find out how to manage it. Learn from others who have the confidence you are missing. Free yourself from result or outcome thinking – focus on how you achieve your goal/task.

I believe people can be extraordinary. Reaching into skills they didn't know existed, and achieving results they never thought possible.

I believe people CAN be extraordinary, the question is, are you one of those people?

See things as you would have them be, instead of as they are.

Robert Collier

The hardest thing to believe when you're young is that people will fight to stay in a rut, but not to get out of it.

Ellen Glasgow

The most powerful agent of change is a change of heart.

Gil Atkinson

We aren't forced to follow the old ideas.

J. George Bendorz

Are you celebrating the good old days or living for the great new ones?

When you are through learning, you are through.

Vernon Law

Change is inevitable; growth is intentional.

Glenda Cloud

The reward for conformity is everyone likes you but yourself.

Rita Mae Brown

LEAVE YOUR COMFORT ZONE. GO STRETCH YOURSELF FOR A GOOD CAUSE.

KOBI YAMADA

Paying attention to your levels of energy and what elements of life create and zap your energy can help you manage energy flows throughout the day for optimum performance. Knowing how to maintain a consistent 'sweet spot' for productivity throughout the course of a day is critical. A simple example is creating something enjoyable on a Monday to be revved up about returning to the working week! Some possibilities that work for me include lunch with friends, a music lesson or a game of squash that night with my mate Disco to get the hotly contested 'title belt'!

I have given an example below of some of the creators and zappers that are true for me. Please don't just read and assess this list, use it as a catalyst to contemplate your own dynamics. Then, simply make sure you have creators surrounding, or at a bare minimum, balancing your zappers, to manage your energy levels throughout the various parts of the day!

CREATORS

- That first morning coffee
- Working with people to generate new ideas
- Getting out for a walk and some oxygen during the day
- Feeling prepared, organized and informed
- Being connected to my team and colleagues
- Lunches, dinners, brunch… getting out for an hour

ZAPPERS

- Hearing problems not possibilities
- Not being aware or managing my time and tasks well
- Poor eating habits, meals on the run or skipped altogether
- A lack of space to contemplate, reflect and learn
- Confronting or dealing with poor communication skills
- Feeling unsupported
- People who lack thought for others

Would you?

What's your attitude to taking risks?

Its not olny srmat poelpe taht can raed tihs. I cdnuolt blveiee taht I cluod aulaclty uesdnatnrd what I was rdanieg.

The phaonmneal pweor of the hmuan mnid, aoccdrnig to a rscheearch at Cmabrigde Uinervtisy, it deosn't mttaer in waht oredr the ltteers in a wrod are, the olny iprmoatnt tihng is taht the frist and lsat ltteer be in the rghit pclae. The rset can be a taotl mses and you can sitll raed it wouthit a porbelm.

Tihs is bcuseae the huamn mnid deos not raed ervey lteter by istlef, but the wrod as a wlohe. Amzanig huh? yaeh and I awlyas tghuhot slpeling was ipmorantt!

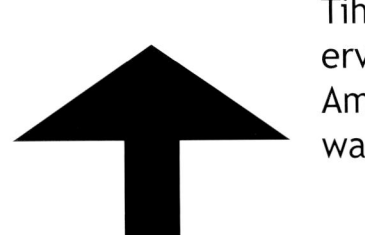

Read This

Think about this

Amazing huh! Maybe there is a learning here about the human condition.

Not everything has to be aligned, in the right order or all bases covered to make sense of something or take action. Are you maximizing life through taking half chances and momentary opportunities, or waiting until the time, mood or circumstances are exactly right before taking action?

OK...OK... I get that some decisions do need consideration; just be sure that not everything in your life has to be completely planned or perfect before exciting opportunities, detours and events can be entertained and explored.

After all, when it comes to your life; are you Chairman of the Board or Chairman of the Bored?

Who controls the decisions and outcomes that matter to you? What is it that you stand for or are known for with friends, colleagues or family?

Part of being content in life is not to always get things your own way, but feel you have control over what matters to you and consequently the decisions you make. The ability to lead yourself in various circumstances, situations and life context is critical to achieve your 'magnetic north' striving to be the best person you can be.

Although leadership is a complex subject that fills many bookstore shelves with models, theories, experiences and recommendations, below are a couple of simple ideas to generate your leadership capability.

What can you do?

- Be on a constant journey of working out what matters to you. What are your day to day actions servicing? What would you speak up or make a stand for and why? Leading yourself is the first step towards success.

- Take the lead – regularly. Commit yourself to at least one leadership act each day. On taking action always take time to reflect on what you did, why you did it and whether you achieved the result you wanted.

- Remember leaders are learners! Your actions don't always have to achieve the desired result to be beneficial!

- Leaders always develop other leaders. Anyone can put people down or make comments or decisions to 'fit in'. Have courage and give time to grow other people, moment to moment and day to day, to be their best!

Are you the leader in your life?

Celebrate adversity right now. Great development and personal growth comes after pushing through tough times. What was your last triumph over adversity?

WHAT'S STOPPING YOU?

We all have decisions that we are putting off or hesitant to make due to the voices in our head reminding us of the negative or potentially frightening things that might happen:

- 🛑 I'll be ridiculed for my idea
- 🛑 People will judge me
- 🛑 I'll be rejected personally
- 🛑 Can I live with the possible rejection?
- 🛑 I don't know if I will succeed
- 🛑 I have never done it before

...the list is endless. Do any of these resonate with you?

Below are a couple of questions to assist you to move your mind around some of the angles involved with challenging decisions:

- 🚦 What's stopping you taking action right now?
- 🚦 What's the worst case scenario that could happen?
- 🚦 What might be possible or created from taking action?
- 🚦 What is it that worries you the most?
- 🚦 How could you minimize your worst case scenario coming true?

DON'T just read through this list aimlessly! Choose a decision and focus on what might be possible. Then, take a breath, inhale some courage, and embrace the opportunity to take life by the collar.

Living with risk, responding to opportunity and growing yourself through new experiences makes life great and people distinctive.

The choice is yours. Do what you have always done or get on your bike and motor through a new experience and opportunity.

Whatchadoin'?

Everyday we consider and make decisions. Sometimes the decisions are easy and sometimes more complex due to a range of possibilities, circumstances and the involvement of other people that add levels of complication.

Whatever decisions are being chosen reflect our personal choice. Often we feel like options don't exist, however choice is always something we have. Who we are determines how we view, understand and make those choices.

I am not just talking about the kind of hypothetical situations suggested in a board game but the everyday decisions you make. The decisions that give your life focus and either promotes the way you want your life to be or moves you away from that place.

Should I go for a run? Alex needs help with the deadline but I promised to be home at 6 pm. I have been invited to a work function but I don't want to attend. I feel guilty about sleeping in. That dress looks stunning but is expensive. I am bored in my job. I feel like a burden on my partner.

How we view life's choices and make decisions, cognizant of what needs we are fulfilling through the choices we make, directly relate to our sense of self and level of happiness.

TRACK AND FIELD LEGEND

"I FOUND longer races boring. I found the mile just perfect."

- Inducted: 2001 -

Do you know this athlete? No? Well we all have a lot to learn from **Roger Bannister.**

Prior to May 6th, 1956 no-one had ever run a sub four minute mile. In fact, the world record of 4:01.3 had been held for nine years promoting the belief that running the mile under the four minute mark was impossible.

History shows that Roger Bannister broke the four minute mile and subsequently the World Record, when he ran a stunning race at the Iffley Road track on the fateful May 6th day. His time was 3:59.4 seconds. So where's the lesson?

Sure, there is a simple message that the seemingly impossible can be achieved. Yet more than that, this story is about belief. Prior to Bannister breaking the mark the record had been held for nine years. Many had tried to conquer the illustrious four minute mile and many came up short.

From Roger Bannister breaking the record how long do you think it took for the record to be broken again? Just forty six days. John Landy broke the record just forty six days later in Finland. Why then did a nine year record get broken again so quickly?

Belief

Athletes, once believing the record was impossible, could now see it could be done. A change of belief directly affects the mindset and consequently the results that can be achieved. Athletes now had a different purpose and focus when they ran.

How are your beliefs about what is possible or not effecting what you go for and achieve?

Are you making a life or making a living?

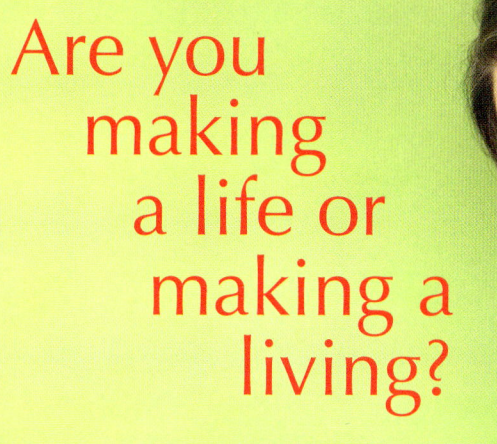

Quite honestly, there is not one correct or desired answer to the above question.

What REALLY matters is that you are a) aware of and b) happy about your response to the above statement. It's easy to fall into patterns that are created for us as opposed to making informed, and at times, courageous choices to create our own patterns.

Use this page to think about your daily routines and habits. What are they servicing for you? Is this what you want? Take stock and ensure whatever your dreams for life – they are being created through the actions and decisions you make every day.

Work like you don't need the money,
  love like you've never been hurt
    and dance like no-one's watching.

Mood swing

There is absolutely no doubt that the way we feel impacts on the way we act.

Yet often, for some strange reason, our mood can lead us to undertake approaches and positions in living life that are restricting and limiting.

Listening and being in tune with yourself is one thing, allowing feelings of laziness, lethargy and general minimal pursuit of life's rewards can often lead to uninspired thinking and low level engagement with people and opportunities.

When was the last time you defied your mood and jumped off the couch when you didn't want to exercise? Started a task that you have been putting off? Or went out when a night at home was beckoning?

Being able to defy your mood at the time that life is calling (and you be the judge of that) will ensure you are living life for the moment, taking opportunities that arise and not being limited solely by how you feel.

So next time your mood is dictating you close one of life's opportunities down – defy it. Do the opposite and take back control of when and what you do.

Do it today and see what happens. You never know what might eventuate.

Where does your mood and approach to life lead you?

You snooze you lose!
What effect is constantly hitting the snooze button having on you?

For most people 'snooze time' is already factored into the calculations of what time the alarm goes off; and how many presses of the snooze button they can have before actually having to get up and start the day. Is this the most restful sleep that can be achieved?

Often with snoozing, time is spent worrying about sleeping through the postponed alarm, and consequently what the time is; how much more 'snooze time' you have and what tasks you could forego (like ironing the shirt or washing your hair) to gain more time to doze.

Whether it is ten minutes or thirty minutes, by snoozing what you are actually losing is that time for restful sleep.

Constantly pressing the alarm, half asleep and half awake creates a drowsy and slow start to any day. For five days try setting the alarm for when you need to get up and eradicate the snoozing altogether. Keep your snoozing or sleeping in to weekends and reap the rewards during the week that a quality and restful sleep can provide.

Just having a browse or are you prepared to invest $29.95 in your own or someone else's future?

Be Careful... This is a Ghost Story!

Not that long ago I caught up with a friend when traveling. We initially decided on lunch but through various reasons and circumstances ended up at a cinema. The only movie we could see due to session times was *The Grudge*. A Japanese horror movie adapted for the English screen. And this is where the story begins.

See, normally when choosing to invest my entertainment dollar a horror movie would not even rate amongst my choices. My friend, however, was very keen to see this movie, so I agreed.

As a 32-year-old grown man at the time, I was continually frightened throughout the movie. My fingers gripped the seat tightly, music cued my anticipation for another scare and the Jaffa's had no chance in my sweaty hands.

Here is the funny thing though. At the end of the movie I found myself on an emotional high as I had just put myself through an experience that I would normally choose to avoid. My body, mind and all associated senses were not used to this experience and I actually found myself enjoying the feeling as a consequence.

I was experiencing emotions similar to post traumatic events when you have 'come through' and realize everything is going to be OK. My heart was racing, my adrenalin pumping; I couldn't help laughing and felt almost euphoric about reaching the end of the movie.

Having this experience after watching a horror film got me thinking. Sure it is easy to make movie decisions based on what I like or preferences I have established, but I hadn't as an adult ever given the horror film genre a chance. I had always made a conscious choice NOT to see horror films.

I couldn't help but wonder what other experiences I had been sheltering myself from through the choices I was making? Once I was conscious to this thought it was amazing how many of my decisions were made from past experience and personal preference as opposed to what might be right or appropriate at that time.

If I ceased operating from autopilot and completely interacted with the world mindfully and with active thought in the way I was living each day, how much more of life could I attempt, experience and value?

I made a decision then and there to be conscious of the choices I make to ensure that whatever I am engaging in day to day is not solely being dictated by habit, previous experience or personal preference. I know from this experience that the preferences I choose may seem right for me but may not always be right for the circumstance; and in fact may just limit my experience.

I am not suggesting you go and see a horror film this weekend! The aim of sharing this story is purely to encourage you to be mindful of the opportunities in your own life, to challenge yourself to go beyond your own preferences. Sure they work for you because they are familiar and comfortable - but are they providing you new challenges, experiences and opportunities to grow your capabilities?

Some of you will take a leap of faith where others will tread carefully with small steps. The approach doesn't really matter. What is the key is that you engage and experience new approaches, if they don't work out, you can always go back to what you know and prefer! Trying something new doesn't necessarily mean a permanent change.

That's the real beauty in living with mindfulness. Doing different things brings new wisdom.

Don't say you don't have time. You have exactly the same number of hours per day that were given to Helen Keller, Pasteur, Michelangelo, Mother Teresa, Leonardo da Vinci, Thomas Jefferson and Albert Einstein.

H Jackson Brown Jnr

THE TRUE BEAUTY of life and living is making the most of what it has to offer. We all have the same amount of time, gifts, talents and possibility, however perhaps not in the same areas or demonstrated in the same ways. When teaching it became evident one year the gifted mathematician envied the great athlete, the great athlete looked favorably toward the skilled artist and the skilled artist craved the freedom of the class's free spirit.

WE OFTEN SEE the best in other people yet rarely allow ourselves the opportunity to recognize and be proud of our own skills and gifts, let alone tap into them! While watching and admiring others' skills from a distance we fail to look inside ourselves to see, respect and access the very talents that make us capable.

FORGET THE QUOTE opposite being about time and see the bigger picture. There are always reasons we could offer ourselves not to do something – time is just one of the largest excuses people provide.

WHAT COULD HAPPEN in your life IF you put aside the reasons, excuses and justifications for doing something a certain way or seeing a certain perspective; escaped your old ideas and ways and made a change?

IS THE POSSIBILITY you are thinking of worth taking action? Then do it. It is as easy and as difficult as that.

I am just not ready

I would NEVER do that!

It's just not for me

I only work here part-time

After you...

What would people think?

No, you listen!

There aren't enough hours in the day...

I'd love to but...

No

Perhaps another time

Sorry...

It's not up to me

WHAT'S YOUR EXCUSE?

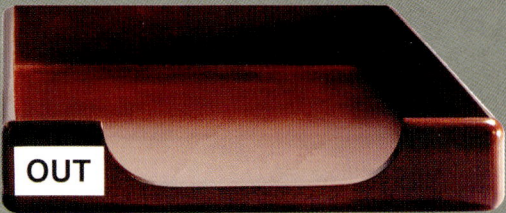

Is this reflective of how you manage time in your life?

GET A GRIP!

Grab a good night's sleep paying attention to your body/habits to know what works in ensuring you get the rest you need.

Get smart about your time. Find out how long your 'day job' job takes each week and remember to include all activity including phone calls, talking to customers and incidentals that often blow out the day.

Once you have an understanding of the hours required you can make more informed choices about your time as things arise.

Learn to say no politely to avoid over committing yourself!

Get up earlier. Well, it is an option!!?

If you are not managing your time who is?

Don't be afraid to ask for help. Struggling with tasks to save face can often be a huge time waster.

Stuck on a task? Don't get bogged down in the battle. Go out for a 10 minute walk and return with fresh eyes and some newly oxygenated blood.

Don't put things off until tomorrow. Start it today!

Write down one thing you feel is out of your control: deadlines, other people, stakeholders and not enough time are common. Spend five minutes brainstorming options YOU have to manage one of those issues. Now you have a list of solutions choose one and go and make it happen! Taking action has moved that thing from out of control to being under your influence - nicely done!

WHEN DID YOU LAST GET AWAY?

When was your last holiday? Not a break, but a genuine holiday?

Sand, sun and surf. Relax, unwind and dine. An exotic adventure with a backpack. Child free. Time at home, together or alone. Domestic touring to see your own country. Trees, breeze and nature. Sleeping in, late breakfasts and a leisurely look over the paper. Exclusive time with your partner. Jobs around the house working with your hands. Day trips and spas, wineries and open fires.

Whatever approach 'blows your hair back' think; when did you last genuinely get away? There is so much good that is gained from taking some time off and welcoming the chance to rejuvenate the heart, mind, body and soul. Our day to day life structures and routines can so easily dominate our existence if we don't take charge.

Allocate some time at the start of the year so that getting away is not a matter of finding time, it's just a matter of taking it. Trust me, you could be as relaxed and carefree as this guy!

Graduated performance

Try something new more than once.

The more you do it, the more it's defined and the easier it gets.

Go ahead... try something new!

This book is hopefully full of thought provokers and good ideas that, to date, have made you think as you have read and interacted with the pages. Problem is, reading is an intellectual exercise.

The real opportunity for learning, growing personally and having impact through new behaviour is actually trying something new. I have consciously avoided giving advice reflective of a one size fits all mentality or approach – however I don't suggest that just reading this book is enough!

Whether you believe in taking a small step toward a different approach OR taking a leap of faith in committing your complete self to a task, do it! Read a page, find the perspective of seeing something differently or an insight to take action but DON'T be passive.

If nothing comes to mind or the suggestions made on some pages don't work for you, read the possibilities opposite to kick off your own thinking… and of course, consequent action!

- Share your thoughts and feelings with a friend over a meal or beverage and get their ideas.

- Talk to your colleagues, your boss, team mates at sport and share your intent with them. Put your development on public record and get people's support.

- Watch a DVD that gives you personal inspiration. Straight after (yeah as the credits roll!) write down whatever ideas come into your head.

- Start by asking yourself what's stopping you from devising possibilities. Understanding the barrier to your thinking might just be the obstacle to overcoming a raft of great ideas and possibilities!

- Find a person who you believe has a skill or characteristic that you don't have. Talk with them and get suggestions about how they developed their skill and currently use them to get some ideas of your own.

- Read on the subject — these days there are books on almost every possible topic covered in these pages. Invest $25 on a book and find out the specifics about that area and what to try.

- Write yourself a letter about what you want to be different and why. Putting pen to paper without needing to show anyone else may stimulate possibilities and actions.

- Find time and space to really think. Not at home or work but a new environment where your mind can be stimulated. By a river, at a café, in a park? wherever!

- Write a list of possible actions to take without worrying about how to do it or what the result may be. Review the list and narrow your selection to four possibilities you ARE prepared to try — then choose one!

- Use the www to search for existing ideas or possibilities!

Go on... take what you deserve (and a little more) in life!

EAT CAKE WITH YOUR COFFEE - ADD SOME CREAM

ROMANCE THE DOONA ANOTHER HOUR THIS WEEKEND

RING A FRIEND AND INVITE YOURSELF AROUND FOR A MEAL

SPEND MONEY ON AN OUTFIT YOU WILL WEAR PROUDLY AND ENJOY

ARE YOU A 70% OR GREATER FIT? THEN GO FOR THAT JOB!

SAY NO TO SOMETHING YOU DON'T FEEL LIKE DOING

SAY THANK-YOU TO A COMPLIMENT RATHER THAN 'DOWNPLAY' IT

BE THE PERSON WHO TAKES THE LAST BISCUIT ON THE PLATE

PUT SOMETHING OFF UNTIL TOMORROW

SAY NO TO YOUR BOSS!

What else?

Excess baggage – everyone's got it...

Just take a peek... don't want a good look.

Unpack it - lay it all out!

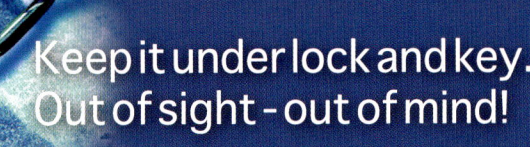

Keep it under lock and key.
Out of sight - out of mind!

…how do YOU manage it?

Load it all up and carry it around?

Grab a porter.
Let someone else carry it!

Just leave it behind.

Do any of these resonate with you?
Are your strategies currently working?

Confronting a new situation or challenge?

Being in conflict with someone?

A decision you made and now regret?

Feeling single and all alone?

Every person has areas of their life that create uncertainty and doubt. Often over-thinking, searching for advice or counsel from others can just exacerbate the issue rather than provide clarity due to the multitude of opinions and perspectives.

One of the keys to effective decision making, and ideally resolution for the things that keep you up at night is to get to the heart of the issue. There are many symptoms that present themselves and create havoc with your thinking if you don't allow yourself the space to access the core issue at hand. Take the simple example of having a headache; do these suggestions sound familiar?

Have a glass of water
Go and lay down for ten minutes
Take an analgesic

Go to the doctor
Grab a cup of coffee
Take a walk and get some fresh air

Although some may have relevance in particular situations, most are responding to the symptom of the headache itself rather than finding out the reason for the headache; the fundamental issue.

Would the responses above be different if you knew the person had interstate visitors that their partner doesn't like, they are suffering from lack of sleep due to entertaining their guests, work pressures are mounting due to tight project deadlines and there is an expectation of needing to be seen to have everything under control?

What keeps you

Finding out the reasons why something exists enables the issue to be managed at its core so a sustainable long-term solution can be found. The alternative is managing symptoms that may provide short-term relief, but will only return because the fundamental issue or cause has ultimately not been addressed.

What can you do? Ask why!

Allow yourself to dig deeper with your thinking and find the real reasons why something is gnawing at you. Ask yourself at least five why's to uncover the issue at hand. Keep going until your responses start to become too broad or do not make sense.

Issue	*I feel really nervous about meeting my new partner's friends*
Why #1	*because I am worried they may not like me*
Why #2	*because I don't feel confident when meeting new people*
Why #3	*I always feel conscious of myself and creating a good impression*
Why #4	*because I want people to think the best of me*
Why #5	*because I want to be liked by people*

So from being nervous and worrying about meeting new people, the fundamental issue seems to be about being liked as opposed to meeting the new partner's friends. This is a much deeper realization. The point in this example is not to find the appropriate solution, but highlight the importance of uncovering the fundamental issue; and how strategies and approaches to address a long-term solution would now very different than just addressing ways of reducing nerves when meeting new people.

awake at night?

> Twenty years from now you'll be more disappointed by the things you didn't do than by the ones you did.
>
> — Mark Twain

Are you failing every now and then?

Each time we stuff something up or reflect upon a decision or action where we would like to go back and do things differently, there is an opportunity for learning.

How we manage this learning experience is crucial to our future success and happiness. Reflecting, sucking the learning juices from the experiences and moving on, is healthy.

Constantly beating yourself up, telling others of your failings or not allowing yourself to absorb the mistake will rot you from the inside.

Seeing learning opportunities as an investment in making you better will assist in absorbing that incident and moving forward. Focusing on the future enables efforts and energy from one experience to another to be harnessed and directed toward your next success.

NASA made 35 failed attempts at launching a rocket before success was achieved. That's 35 experiences of nothing but failure!

The key therefore is about how much failure you can tolerate and checking your preparedness to fail every now and then to keep learning as a person.

Zig Ziglar said that if you are not failing every now and then you are playing it safe. When was YOUR last failure?

Are you sick of your spare tyre?
Doing anything about it?

adaptive thinking

A lot of circumstances or issues that occur in life have technical or known solutions.

You break your arm for example. You head to the doctor who determines the type and severity of the break, provides a diagnosis and then sets the arm in plaster. With physiotherapy and time for recovery, the outcome for the patient, like the other steps in this process is known.

There is however some issues that we confront where the solution is still unknown.

A potentially controversial example is the situation in the Middle East. Does anyone know the true issues surrounding this situation; is it oil, politics, religion? Without knowing the issue, the diagnosis and consequent action also remain unknown. In this situation adaptive and creative thinking is required.

The page opposite gives a simple framework to access your creative and adaptive thinking skills when you find yourself needing some ideas for unknown situations in your own life.

Identify the issue

What is the issue?
How are you impacted?
When did it begin?
How did it start?
Who or what is involved?

Generate possibilities (not answers - possibilities)

Make a list of all the possibilities that enter into your head as a way of creating a solution.

Have fun with this and don't edit your thoughts just yet. At this stage they are all good!

Just get them all down.

What works for you?

Go back over your list and now edit for what excites you, what's realistic and possible. What will be a good resolution without hurting someone else?

Take action!

Your now edited list only has possible solutions.

Choose the action that best meets your needs and intent in resolving your issue.

If you still have a long list be tough and make a shortlist of the three best ideas.

Action your #1 idea.

Welcome the **task** that makes you go beyond yourself.

FRANK MCGEE

Think about one aspect of your life that you want to be different. How are you creating that change? One of the major barriers to effective change is by desiring change without your own input, action, taking calculated risks or making choices and sacrifices. Change does not occur by managing the status quo, shying away from conversations or ignoring the power of personal choice and impact. The power for changing your circumstances has to be greater than the resistance to that change for anything meaningful to happen.

Create change in your life

Why are you dissatisfied?	What needs to be different?	How will YOU create it?
What is it that you want to change?	What does the new situation look like?	What are the steps you need to take?
Why is the situation not working now?	How does it feel and/or operate for you?	Who do you need to approach?
What is it about your current situation that makes you unhappy?	How would this improve for the other person or people involved?	How will you gain support for the change?
How would it look in the future if you didn't do anything?	What would the impact of successful change be for you?	Who else needs to be engaged or involved?
What impact does this situation have on other areas of your life?	Are there other options available to you?	Where will you go to gain encouragement and support to keep up your energy levels?
What is the core thing that you are dissatisfied with?	Do these excite or interest you? Why?	Do you have the necessary resources?
How would life be if this situation or your feelings of dissatisfaction did not exist?	What do you want to create as an outcome?	Is the change realistic and possible?
Is there anything you need to change?	What are the possible results of you taking action?	How will you know the change is finished?
		How will you celebrate once you have been successful?

What are the reasons for your resistance? What stops you taking action?

Some simple steps to create change and in the process evaluate your own thinking as to how your desire for change is matched against the resistance to make that change. Should you swing that equation (if necessary) and make your desire for the change greater than the resistance you will have success. Success builds on success so continuing creating change to fulfill your own life and happiness.

Are you paying attention to life's little treasures? Life is a rich tapestry of experiences as minor as eating lunch in the sun to major events such as the birth of your first child. Being alive and conscious to life and the richness it provides each and every day is a gift in itself. When was the last time you got off your daily treadmill to open your eyes and appreciate one of life's little treasures?

Our lives today seem full of being so busy that simple elements of a gifted and generous life often pass us by. Cloudiness can set in when our lives become in service of needing to achieve, pursuing material wealth and generally gathering more 'stuff'. Stuff that often represents other things we desire or feelings we crave such as a sense of belonging, approval or self worth.

When did you last appreciate your child's seemingly simple achievement, throw a few coins to a busker for providing a brief moment's entertainment, appreciate the real flavors of a fine meal or recognise the closeness of friends to share a success with or lean on during a distressing time in your life?

Take a moment and remind yourself of the little treasures you can access in life. The things that take time but if you are not mindful of can so often be missed. In doing so I hope you reflect to ensure that a) your little treasures are being noticed; and b) if not, you do whatever is necessary to find time to appreciate the little treasures that are part of your life every day.

What is it that you are busy doing?

Faced with the choice between changing one's mind and proving that there is no need to do so, almost everybody gets busy on the proof.

John Kenneth Galbrath
– *American Economist*

What are you hiding?

Ever been in a conversation where you have feelings that don't reflect what you actually say, think about throttling someone or just imagine giving it to them with both barrels? Well be assured you are not alone! Tapping into your true thoughts and feelings - your 'hidden conversation' - could just be the tonic you need to not only keep your sanity; but actually improve the depth and outcome of your conversation. Hidden conversations often hold the thoughts, feelings and emotions that really matter to us as individuals; often adding real value to a conversation by others knowing what you think and how you feel.

Rather than hiding your thoughts, bringing them to a conversation in a respectful way can prove very powerful. Of course in advocating your thoughts and feelings it is also important to engage and encourage the other person through inquiring of their perspective or opinion.

This process of advocacy and inquiry aids in managing conversations that promotes more effective outcomes.

Can you see how these possibilities could make a difference?

"I am feeling frustrated that we don't seem to be moving forward with our ideas; how is everyone else feeling?"

"Jenny that comment came across as accusatory and was quite hurtful; was that how it was intended?"

"I don't feel like the movies tonight but would be happy to go later in the week; would that suit you?"

What are the benefits?

- ❖ The conversation reaches the heart of people and issues being discussed
- ❖ Being open, honest and true to your thoughts, feelings and observations promotes trust
- ❖ Points of misunderstanding, difference or tension are raised in the moment and shared openly
- ❖ Less time is spent second guessing, worrying or percolating over comments and 'conversation replays'
- ❖ The conversation does not 'go somewhere else' which can be unhealthy and prevent relationships being forged through difference

In the acknowledgements for this book I mentioned DtC. A bunch of mates that get together once a month to try the many things life has to offer, and share each others company.

Our activities vary due to the diversity of this group's experiences and interests. Some of our events to date have involved learning to surf, going to live theatre, touring our city's many great restaurants and bars as well as an evening on the bay on a fishing charter.

Of course during these activities time is spent as people. Talking through the success and distress in our lives, sharing perspective of recent community, political or social issues and sharing time that enables learning through doing.

Every month DtC provides an opportunity to attempt something new, challenge and be challenged; and embrace life and its many experiences and opportunities.

DtC is just one of the outlets I have in my life that provides, sometimes in the one night, the opportunity to access and enhance all my intelligences; emotional, intellectual, spiritual and physical.

Most people have an acute awareness of IQ and EQ; however the other intelligences are also critical. It is worth saying here that spiritual intelligence does not necessarily equate directly to holding a particular religion or faith.

Like many things, achieving a balance is critical for a rounded and fulfilling lifestyle. Although each of us has strengths in some areas more than others, developing a rounded personality through choice and action is essential.

Are you creating opportunities in your life to explore and develop the depth and breadth of your intelligence?

EQ

IQ

SQ

PQ

Bounce Back

At some time in our life we will all encounter times of absolute challenge, hardship and difficulty. It is natural to feel deflated and at times upset.

The key with hardship or adversity is about overcoming. People on reflection, will often communicate great learning, sense of achievement or personal growth in having encountered and overcome challenges they have met in life.

A colleague of mine recounts how being diagnosed with Type II diabetes, the doctor demanded changes to his lifestyle. Although initially difficult, having to watch his diet, get regular exercise, give up smoking and make other lifestyle changes actually created a healthier, happier person. Something he said would not have occurred without being confronted by diabetes and the doctor's demands.

We are all different and will see degrees of challenge differently. The key is not in making judgment. In the scheme of life it is what you believe and have done that matters. Be mindful about your own circumstance and perspective.

How you are working with the challenges confronting you right now?

Marionette or MAGNIFICENT?

You create what you have in life. Sure there are external things that impact on life, however it is you who interacts with those factors, weighs options, clarifies intended outcomes, reflects upon previous experiences and ultimately, makes a decision. Work back late, take the kids out to the movies, surprise your partner with a fancy meal at home, ignore a phone call, distance yourself from a team decision… the list is endless.

The first challenge here is to see and accept the connection between how your life is running and the choices you make day to day. Your decisions **ARE** the barometer for your own life. Whether you are reading this feeling good or completely miserable in life, you can pretty much be sure the decisions you have made until now, and those you will make in the future, will determine your view.

Don't think for a second it is being suggested this is easy or sometimes without significant risk or consequence. Yet, this is the beauty of engaging and living life – living with the choices we make, riding the waves of success and responding to setbacks and sometimes failure.

The marionette puppet comes alive when someone else grabs hold of the strings. The skilled operator makes the puppet move, dance, bend and entertain. Problem is, in real life often the decisions we make can be dictated by others as we fail to engage in the thoughts behind our decisions and fail to recognise the connection to the larger picture concerning our happiness.

Take time to reflect upon the decisions you have made today already. Did the choices you make reflect your thoughts, feelings, needs and values? Don't get caught providing excuses either! There are always ways to justify your current actions and provide reasons for your choices and behaviour. Now is your time to be honest with yourself about the needs your decisions are fulfilling – to be liked, accepted into the culture, get ahead in the company, manage the perfect house, be seen as a perfect wife – and understand who is in control of your life.

After all – don't you want to know if you are a marionette or MAGNIFICENT?

Inquiring   Self aware   Wise   Happy   Open to learning   Flexible

Left margin: Strong · Open · Excited · Energised · Creative · Empowered

Right margin: Enthusiastic · Impressionable · Agreeable · Able to make choices

Listen Up!

Have you REALLY been listening?

Have a read of the list below and see if you are guilty of any of these conversation blockers when someone else is talking...

- Not asking questions to understand the other perspective – even if you disagree with it!
- Being distracted by the environment, other things on your mind and passers by...
- Not having or holding some form of eye contact
- Missing body language like nodding, leaning forward or ah humming to show your interest
- Clarify your understanding to check what is said is what is meant – getting a common language
- Thinking and forming your own rebuttal, argument or reasons for a position
- Changing issues all the time to come back to your perspective or ideas

We do not need ears the size of rabbits to get this right!

Just be open to minimizing these blockers, become a genuine listener to see the enormous possibilities of effective and productive conversations.

Me and my boxer shorts

Great thoughts and ideas can come in the most opportune times; for me it invariably occurs as I drift closer to a restful and peaceful sleep. Not wanting to lose the idea or have my sleep interrupted, I reach over to the bedside drawer, grab the closest pair of boxers and throw them towards the bedroom door where I will see them in the morning. As I launch the undergarment I also call out whatever I want to remember out loud and this technique seems to be all I need to commit it to memory.

Next morning I see the boxer shorts on the floor and by association remember the great idea. Now, at a better time because I have had my good nights sleep, I can record whatever may have kept me tossing and turning or been lost altogether overnight. I do this for work ideas, conversations, task lists, reminders; anything that pops into my head and needs to be addressed.

Whether boxers are your undergarment of choice, or at close range, find a technique that works for you to capture when your mind speaks to you; and maybe, just maybe, you might also get a great nights sleep in the process!

Watching Wimbledon this year I saw on the broadcasts that Serena Williams had written reminders and affirmative notes on her hand.

Each statement, although small to fit on her hand, provided a reminder or important message to be lived out on the court; for that particular opponent and supporting her quest to "go all the way".

Shower Power is a great technique to give yourself those affirmations or reminders; taking them out of your subconscious and into your conscious mind.

Statistically, people who write down or record their goals dramatically increase the probability of achieving them.

Imagine what could happen in your life if you not only wrote them down, but reminded yourself of them each and every day?

Shower Power is basic but outstandingly effective. Just write down your goals on a sheet of paper, laminate that sheet (OK so it costs you $1) and stick it in your shower! That's all there is to it!

Then… every morning as you get clean, read over your goals or affirmative statements for yourself.

Achievement does not involve luck but probability. The more you think and act upon your goals, the higher the probability you have of achieving what you desire.

Whether that's a new job, self confidence, great relationship or financial independence, write down where you want to focus your efforts.

Each time you get clean, you are also taking time to get clarity and confidence about achieving what is important to you.

WHAT IF YOU **DIED** YESTERDAY?

Financial planners sometimes use this question to make people think about the implications should the worse case scenario eventuate.

Of course asking this question retrospectively avoids the uneasiness of not knowing what the future holds for any one person.

It does provide an interesting perspective as a question however due to its finality. When realising that time is of the essence and there are not many more days to be alive, it is amazing how priorities, decisions, actions and what is deemed important changes.

Don't wait for the accident or worse case scenario to eventuate to live the life you desire; create and live that life each and every day.

Learn a musical instrument, call your high school sweetheart, tell someone you love them, book that holiday, get fit, turn off your blackberry, read that book, give up smoking.

The point? Make sure what's important to you but can easily be put off or under prioritised has time in your life **today.**

Stocktaking your life ~ where are you at?

How are your levels of energy for tasks ahead?

How are/can you identify and create your life's happiness?

Imagine your life was a see-saw.

How does the view look in relation to its balance?

If you reflected on all parts of your life in the past month - what was it all in service of?

Had any time for yourself lately?

What will YOUR future success look like and how will it be measured?

Don't be limited by these questions ~ keep reflecting and thinking!

Luke Rhinehart was a psychiatrist from the seventies that invented Dice Living. An anarchic world where numbers on a dice corresponded with six options that virtually eliminated the value and benefit of personal choice.

I don't endorse Dice Living but do believe being open and trying new approaches and taking opportunities in life is important. This doesn't need to be complicated either - check out some simple ways to start here…

➤ When next ordering food at a restaurant choose the item that first appeals even before reading the remainder of the menu.

➤ Go without your iPod on the next opportunity to fill your senses and enhance your complete awareness of whatever situation you are engaging in.

➤ Have a 'doona day' this weekend by sleeping late, turning off all contact to the world and really relax.

➤ For one entire day offer a smile to every person that you happen to make eye contact with.

➤ Keep some change in your pocket. When someone who is not as fortunate as you asks for a hand then give them a couple of dollars or even better - buy them a take-away meal.

➤ Do nothing. Sometimes 'busyness' creeps into our lives and never leaves. Get some me or we time.

These are just some starting suggestions as thought provokers. Don't be limited or critical if these don't blow your hair back. Do you see the point? Decide what works for you, what you will do and have some fun doing it!

What does your ideal week look like?

How are YOU making time for the

Wodayawant?

Is what you have in life right now making you happy? The friends that you see and socialize with, the expectations and challenges you confront every day, enjoying the quality time spent with your family, the opportunities to relax and unwind… are these things reflective of what you want to spend your life doing?

If you haven't worked this out by now it is YOU who controls your life and its future direction. Not without sacrifice and consequence but your behavior is always in service of something. Once you work out what that is and align your actions to where you want your life to be, your day to day interaction with the world will be enhanced expedientially.

Why enhanced? Glad you asked. Quite simply (yet really it is difficult to achieve) because you will have control back in your life by being mindful and consequently able to manage your life: from emotions and how you respond to circumstances, career decisions and choices to environments where currently you feel powerless or uninspired.

Unless you are reading this book on morphine one of the pages will have already sparked some recognition and intention about areas of your life. The last part of this book is about trying to assist you move from thinking to doing. Thinking is powerful and has purpose, yet is an intellectual exercise and will not evoke change in your life.

What do you have NOW?

If you want to know your past, look into your present conditions; if you want to know your future, look into your current actions.

Unknown

Our lives are a direct response of who we are. This encompasses all of your life experiences that shape who you are today – family upbringing, social environment and culture, country of origin, education and work experience – literally all of your current life experiences.

If you are living a full life this will continue to change as you grow older and experience different things. You may travel through different countries and cultures, experience the pain and grief of death, have success and achievement through adversity; our ability to continue learning and sharing within humanity is the gift of life.

What is it that you have now in your life? Look back on the pages that resonated with you and ask yourself why? Are there things you are proud of or areas that have provoked your mind's interest due to sensing the need for change? Don't be limited to the pages of this book either. Let your mind reflect on your life to date and note areas where you are happy, areas where you have further questions and areas where you would definitely make change.

Remember that your life and the experiences you have are a barometer for who you are as a person and the way you see and interact with the world. Be mindful not to justify your actions through someone or something else – allocating rather than owning responsibility will only perpetuate the myth that your life, success and happiness is determined by others.

It is only through this level of thinking that you will find the true reasons for what you have in life today. Once you have worked out what your life is in service of right now – or the areas for change you would like to address – there exists a foundation for change.

Thought provokers...

- What is it about your life you enjoy?
- What makes you unhappy or stressed?
- What gives you energy for engaging with and living life?
- How often do you feel energized as opposed to stressed?
- Is your life the way you want it to be?
- How do you get up and greet most mornings?
- How much of your life experiences are 'because of' someone or something else?
- Are you ready and willing to realize that you have choices and can take charge of your life?

Behold the turtle - he only makes progress when he sticks his neck out.

James Conan Bryant

what do YOU want?

Just like visiting a new country and trying to find your way somewhere the first thing you often work out is where you are. It provides a common point to then work out directions to get to where you want to be. Thinking about and reflecting on what your life is today has simply provided the starting point for your journey.

This journey will be difficult due to human nature prompting us to categorise and name things in order to make sense of them. While this is largely helpful in generating a common language and order, it also limits thinking as people justify, reason and sometimes fight for life continuing to be the way it works for them. The thing here is this: generally it is what we know that limits us as people. We are so busy seeing and fighting for things to be our own way that we shelter our experiences, views and possibilities from those that differ from our own.

Creating the life that you want involves taking responsibility and believing that how you see, interact and manage situations has a direct correlation to your outcomes. So at this point think about what it is that you want in life? What do you want to change? This task is harder said than done so a couple of suggestions have been provided to start your thinking. If one fits with your enthusiasm then go for it… otherwise find and choose your own method for reflection.

- **Go for a walk or bike ride and think about it**
- **Ask yourself deep down - why do I do what I do?**
- **Write a list or letter to yourself about exactly what you want from life**
- **Think of times when you have been happy in life and reflect what is common to those times**
- **Talk to someone close to you about what you are trying to achieve and let them help through a meaningful conversation!**
- **Don't forget to think with balance – this isn't about one area of your life but the complete package**
- **Start by listing people you admire in life and why**
- **Get away for a day or weekend to be in a quiet or different environment to aid your thinking**

Please don't make the fatal mistake of thinking how you can or can't achieve what you want. This will limit your reflective and creative process and cause a barrier to your thinking. Just dump it all down! Working out timeframes, priorities, reality checking your desires and the like can all be done later.

The quote at the top of this page is important because sticking your neck out here will involve some risk. Thinking deeply about what you want will create some tensions and emotions that will prevent creative thought. Absorb the feeling, be mindful of the barriers to your thoughts but stay on track; what does life look like for you in creating exactly what you want?

what are YOU going to do?

The secret of health for both mind and body is not to mourn the past, not to worry about the future, nor to anticipate troubles; but to live the present moment wisely and earnestly.

Buddha

The intent of this book is to promote a sense of mindfulness about your life and discover areas where celebration and deliberation balance to create the life you want to lead. The previous two pages (and we're getting close to the end now) focused on stimulating your thinking about what your life is in service of now and what you want it to be in the future.

Now that you know what you want, what else do you need to go out and get it?

Assurance, timelines to keep you on track, a buddy to assist your change process... whatever you need it is now up to you to get through living with mindfulness and presence in each and every moment. For it is in these day to day moments where you clarify perspective, see opportunity and make your choices that determine your life.

Consciousness to what you are indeed creating through each and every interaction in life is a gift. It is the type of gift where in being conscious to your thought, actions, interrelationships and decisions you will see the paths of the most and least resistance. Being distinctive in creating the life that you want and that is important to you, is about taking the lead for your own life, and making the decisions that are right and true for you.

Whatever has resonated for you in reading this book, take action. Start today: with a conversation, a phone call, buying a book to read, make a plan to address your area of need... whatever you have identified, do it!

You have contemplated what you have in life now, you have thought about, written or talked to others to discover what you want for your life – all that remains is to start the journey.

Look famous
Be legendary
Appear complex
Act easy
Radiate presence
Travel lightly
Seem a dream
Prove real

Want more?

People have vast amounts of capability and distinction that exists within them that largely lies untapped for many varied and often complicated reasons.

Designer Learning is passionate about working with individuals, teams, community and corporate organisations that have a desire to find and access their inner capability.

Finding the ability to soar using skills and knowledge that already exist inside people generates substantial benefits to those willing to walk that journey.

If you have enjoyed what you have read in *Check Up from the Neck Up* and want to explore accessing your own or organisation's existing distinction, all you have to do is get in touch.

The step you take today could generate the results you seek tomorrow.

designerlearning@telstra.com